FRESH WATER

Jill Sherman

Enslow Publishing
101 W. 23rd Street
Suite 240
New York, NY 10011
USA
enslow.com

Words to Know

cleansers Mixtures used to clean different things.

crops Plants that are grown for food.

ingredient Something in a mixture.

natural resource Something from nature that people use.

poison A substance that can cause animals or people to get very sick or die.

recycle To reuse or make something new.

sewage Waste carried away in sewers.

CONTENTS

Water, Water Everywhere

Water is everywhere. It collects in lakes and rivers. Turn on the tap. It flows right into your home. It even falls from the sky as rain!

FAST FACT
Water covers more than 70 percent of Earth.

Water to Live

Water is a natural resource. People, animals, and plants need water to live. Only fresh water is safe to drink. Fresh water is in lakes, rivers, and ice. It is under the ground, too.

Water to Grow

Crops need water to grow. The water comes from rain. Or farmers bring the water themselves. Without water we would not have food.

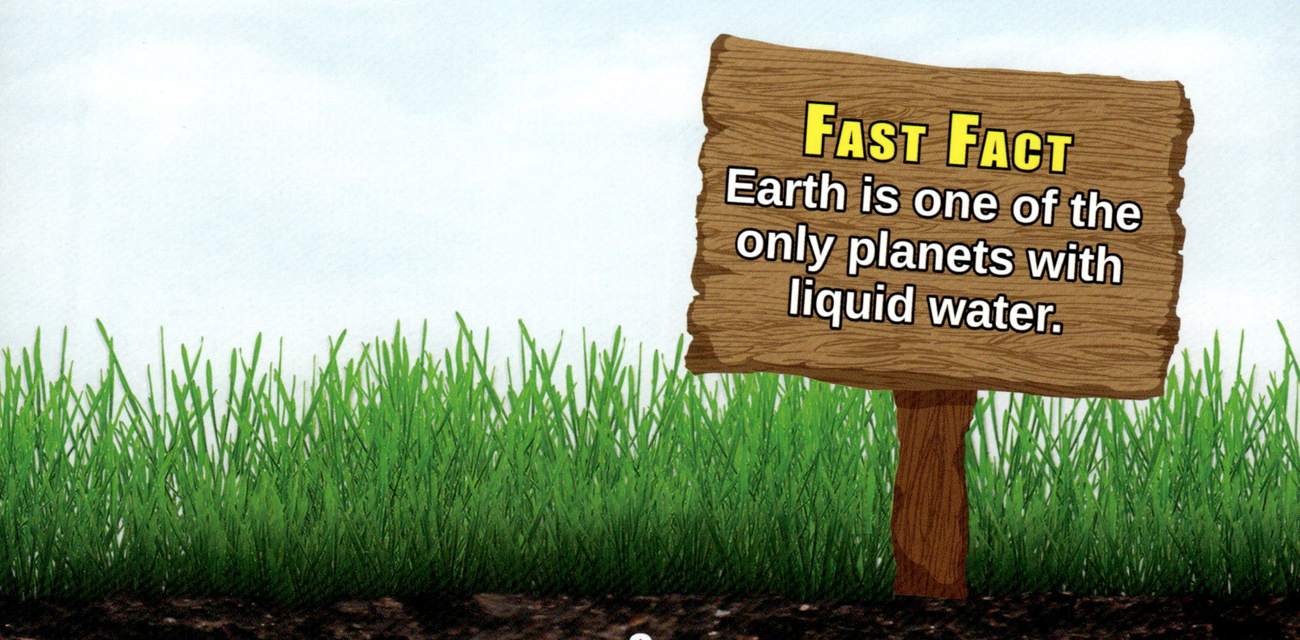

Water in Your Home

We also use water to cook. Boil it for pasta. Mix it into cake batter. Stir it into soups. Water turns ingredients into a tasty meal.

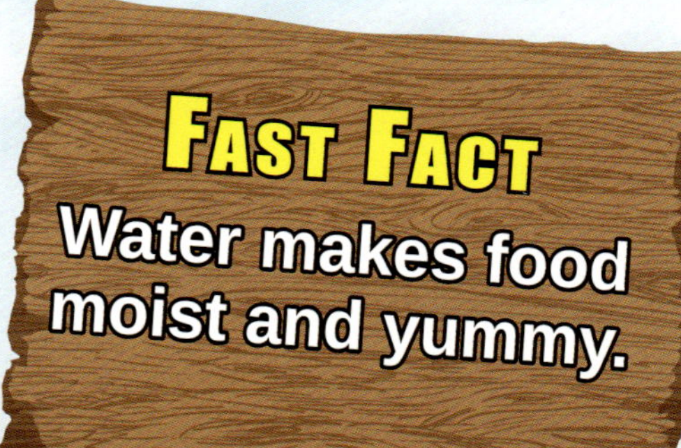

Keep It Clean

What else do you do with water? Clean! Mix with soap to make suds. Now take a bath. Wash the car. Mop the floor. Wash away the dirt.

FAST FACT
Water is an ingredient in many **cleansers**.

Summer Fun

It's hot outside. Time to cool off. Take a dip in the pool. Visit a water park. Go on a boat ride. Water cools our bodies. And it is great to play and relax.

FAST FACT

Surfing, swimming, and boating are great water sports to enjoy.

Making Things with Water

We need water to make things. It is an important ingredient. We use it when we make paper. We use it to dye fabric. There are few things that water has not touched.

Wasted Water

Some water is too dirty to drink.
Crops are sprayed with poisons.
Businesses dump their waste.
Cities flush their sewage. It gets into the water supply. People become sick.

Use Water Wisely

We must not use too much water. Nature cannot recycle water any faster. And we cannot tell nature where to rain. We need fresh water for the future.

Fast Fact

Your family uses about 400 gallons of water per day. Recycle water by watering your plants with cooking water.

Activity

Watch the Tap

Procedure:

1. Place a notebook and pencil near each sink in your home.

2. Ask every person in your home to write down every time they use the

sink. Have them write what they used the water for.

3. Collect the notebooks after one day.

4. How many times did your family use water in one day? What does your home use tap water for the most?

5. What other places in your home use water? Washing machines, dishwashers, hoses, and toilets use water.

LEARN MORE

Books

Bright, Michael. *From Raindrop to Tap.* New York, NY: Crabtree Publishing, 2016.

Enz, Tammy. *Liquid Planet: Exploring Water on Earth with Science Projects.* North Mankato, MN: Capstone Publishers, 2016.

Mulder, Michelle. *Every Last Drop: Bringing Clean Water Home.* Custer, WA: Orca Book Publishers, 2014.

Websites

US Environmental Protection Agency
www3.epa.gov/watersense/kids
This website shows many ways to save water.

US Geological Survey Water Science School
water.usgs.gov/edu/watercycle-kids-adv.html
Learn more about the water cycle with this interactive diagram.

Water Use It Wisely
wateruseitwisely.com/kids
Explore games, adventures, and water-saving tips for kids.

Published in 2018 by Enslow Publishing, LLC.
101 W. 23rd Street, Suite 240, New York, NY 10011

Library of Congress Cataloging-in-Publication Data

Names: Sherman, Jill, author.
Title: Fresh water / Jill Sherman.
Description: New York : Enslow Publishing, 2018. | Series: Let's learn about natural resources | Includes bibliographical references and index. | Audience: K to grade 3.
Identifiers: LCCN 2017018167| ISBN 9780766092358 (library bound) | ISBN 9780766094482 (pbk.) | ISBN 9780766094499 (6 pack)
Subjects: LCSH: Fresh water—Juvenile literature. | Water conservation—Juvenile literature.
Classification: LCC QH541.5.F7 S54 2018 | DDC 577.6—dc23

LC record available at https://lccn.loc.gov/2017018167

Printed in China

Photo Credits: Cover, p. 1 Santiago Urquijo/Getty Images; interior pages background Andrey_Kuzmin/Shutterstock.com; p. 4 TinnaPong/Shutterstock.com; p. 6 EastVillage Images/Shutterstock.com; p. 8 Federico Rostagno/Shutterstock.com; p. 10 CKP1001/Shutterstock.com; p. 12 gorillaimages/Shutterstock.com; p. 14 Varina C/Shutterstock.com; p. 16 Phovoir/Shutterstock.com; p. 18 Shchipkova Elen/Shutterstock.com; p. 20 matka_Wariatka/Shutterstock.com.